Marco Marker
He's a joker who loves messing about, but he always means well, even if he sometimes gets things wrong.
AF469678
Waxy Max
He's very sporty and football mad. On the outside, he's tough, but underneath he's got the biggest heart.
Philippa Feltpen
A real peacemaker, she helps keep the other Pens in order by sorting out arguments and giving good advice.
Splodge, thank you for being so 'splodgy' …
Squiggle and Splodge
The Scribble twins! They're both quiet, both shy. Although they may not look alike, they do almost everything together.
Enter …

Squiggle, your eyebrows are amazing!
Pens
Helping you to get to know God more
Thank YOU God
Mmmm, I suppose they are.
Written by
Alexa Tewkesbury
Every day a short Bible reading is brought to life with the help of the Pens characters. A related question and prayer apply this to daily life. Written in four sections, two focusing on the lives of Pens and two on Bible characters, young children will be inspired to learn more of God and His Word.

What's inside?

CWR

Day 1
EVERY GOOD THING
'You will have all you want to eat, and you will give thanks to the LORD your God ...' (Deuteronomy 8 v 10)
All sorts
Denzil was excited.
Wow!
4

Philippa had helped him to plant vegetables in his garden. Today was the day he had picked his very first runner beans.

Charlotte was delighted.

'Whee!' she squealed.

Philippa had shown her how to grow fruit. Today was the day Charlotte had tasted her very first strawberry.

Max was happy.

'Wahoo!' he whooped.

Philippa had gone shopping with him to buy what he needed to do some baking. Today was the day he'd baked his very first cake.

'God doesn't just give us food,' Philippa smiled. 'He gives us ALL SORTS of food.'

 God gives us different foods to enjoy.

If you were going to grow some fruit and vegetables, what would you choose to plant?

Pens Prayer

For tasty food I can grow, for scrumptious food I can buy – thank You, Lord. Amen.

'May the LORD bless you and take care of you …'
(Numbers 6 v 24)

Pens were getting ready. They'd won the prize for the 'Best Kept Street in Pens' Town' and, to celebrate, they were having a street party.

Marco and Gloria were hanging up flags.

Philippa and Max were blowing up balloons.

Squiggle and Splodge were setting out tables and chairs.

Denzil and Charlotte were putting out the food.

Sharpy was running up and down, sniffing hungrily.

'I'm glad we live in THIS street,' beamed Marco, happily. 'Our houses have stripy bits and spotty bits and the brightest colours in the whole of Pens' town. I wouldn't want to live anywhere else.'

 It's important to thank God for the homes we live in.

What do you like most about where you live?

Pens Prayer

Dear Father, I'm sad that some people don't have a proper home. I want to thank You right now for mine. Amen.

Every Good Thing

'Two are better off than one, because together they can work more effectively.' (Ecclesiastes 4 v 9)

Together

One morning, Squiggle said, 'Let's go for a walk.'

'Where shall we walk *to*?' asked Splodge.

'The beach,' smiled Squiggle.

'I LOVE the beach,' giggled Splodge.

After a while, Squiggle said, 'Let's have a snack.'

'What shall we snack *on*?' asked Splodge.

'Chocolate biscuits,' grinned Squiggle.

'I LOVE chocolate biscuits,' laughed Splodge.

When they'd wandered along the beach and back again, Squiggle said, 'Let's go home and watch TV.'

'What shall we watch?' asked Splodge.

'Something funny,' suggested Squiggle.

'I LOVE funny things!' beamed Splodge. 'And most of all, I love it when we do things TOGETHER.'

God loves to see us share special times with our families and friends.

Next time you're with one of your friends, what could you do together?

Pens Prayer

Loving Lord, thank You so much for giving us each other. Amen.

Every Good Thing

'Remember the LORD in everything you do ...'
(Proverbs 3 v 6)

Sharpy ran … jumped … and caught it in his mouth!

'Wahaay, Sharpy!' cried Max. 'That was AWESOME! Bet you can't do it again!'

He kicked the ball up into the air once more. This time it went higher. So high, it looked as if it was going to fly over the fence!

'Oops!' muttered Max.

But Sharpy ran … jumped … and caught it in his mouth – again!

'You're AMAZING, Sharpy,' laughed Max.

Sharpy panted happily. He rather liked being called amazing.

 **God gives us the ability to learn to do AMAZING things.**

Can you throw a ball in the air and catch it? What about throwing and catching a ball with someone else?

Pens Prayer

Father God, for being able to learn to do different things – I thank You. Amen.

Every Good Thing

'… my God will supply all your needs.' (Philippians 4 v 19)

The new wardrobe

Gloria was going to buy a new wardrobe.

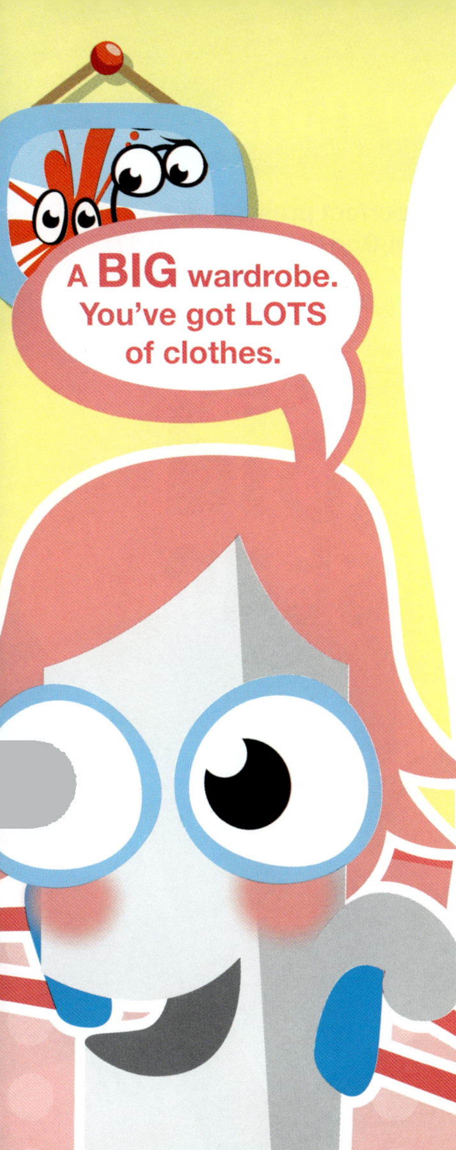

'I *have*,' agreed Gloria.

'You've got a beautiful coat,' Charlotte said.

'To keep me snug *outside*,' nodded Gloria.

'You've got some cosy jumpers,' Charlotte said.

'To keep me snug *inside*,' answered Gloria.

'You've got some pretty dresses,' Charlotte said.

'To make me feel nice wherever I am,' smiled Gloria.

'You've got SO MANY hats!' Charlotte said.

'To dress up my head!' beamed Gloria. 'Isn't it wonderful having things to wear?'

 God knows we need clothes to be comfortable every day.

Pens Prayer

Dear Lord God, thank You for my clothes that keep me warm in winter and cool in summer. Amen.

Day 6
Every Good Thing
'Every good gift and every perfect present comes from heaven; it comes down from God …' (James 1 v 17)
marco's gold star
Marco's writing book
14

When Marco got home from school one Friday, he was feeling clever.

'I've learnt LOADS this week,' he grinned to himself.

On the first day of the week, he'd learnt how to add up some big numbers.

On the second day, he'd learnt how to spell some big words.

On the third day, he'd written his first poem.

On the fourth day, he'd painted a splendid picture.

On the last day, his teacher stuck a gold star in his writing book because he'd worked so hard.

'I *love* school,' he said. 'I wonder what I'll be learning next week.'

 Going to school means we can be taught to do lots of new things.

What do you like doing most at your school or preschool?

Pens Prayer

Father, thank You so much for schools and preschools. Being taught something new is like being given a present! Amen.

Day 7
Every Good Thing
'… he gives you rain from heaven …' (Acts 14 v 17)
Wild about water
16

Denzil was hot. Boiling hot.

Denzil's mouth was dry. Bone dry.

He'd been out on his bike in the blazing sunshine.

'I'm having a shower,' he puffed.

The water washed him off and cooled him down.

'I'm so thirsty, I must have a drink,' he said.

He took a big gulp from a mug of water. It was cold and refreshing.

Philippa smiled, 'I'm going to the beach, Denzil. Come with me.'

She and Denzil ran into the sea. The salty water made them tingle.

'I'm WILD about water!' Denzil cried. 'There are so many ways to enjoy it!'

 God gives us the water we need and water to have fun in, too.

We use water in lots of different ways. How many can you think of?

Pens Prayer

Thank You, heavenly Lord, for Your wonderful gift of water. Amen.

Day 8
Every Good Thing
'May God, the source of hope, fill you with all joy and peace …' (Romans 15 v 13)
Story worlds
I've just been in a castle and hidden from a giant!
18

'I've just been in the woods and run away from a wolf!' shrieked Squiggle.

'I've just been in the jungle and talked to a tiger!' gasped Charlotte.

She'd taken Squiggle and Splodge to the library and they'd been looking at books all afternoon.

They'd read stories crammed with excitement.

They'd read stories full of danger.

They'd read stories that made them laugh and think and wonder.

'Aren't stories BRILLIANT?' beamed Charlotte, her eyes sparkling. 'Every time you read one, you step into another world!'

There are lots of imaginative ways to enjoy the days God gives us.

Do you like looking at books? Which story world do you like stepping into the most?

Pens Prayer

For stories that take me to exciting places and for the people who read them with me – I thank You, Father God. Amen.

Every Good Thing

'… the people were full of joy because God had made them very happy.' (Nehemiah 12 v 43)

Each and every day

Gloria had a pile of old magazines.

'I'm not sure what to do with them,' she said.

'Let's cut out pictures of things we like,' suggested Marco. 'We could stick them on a piece of paper to remind ourselves of how much we have to thank God for.'

Pens cut out pictures of a hat and a bicycle; a football and some dog biscuits; a piano, a skateboard, some flowers and a toy box.

When they'd stuck them on the paper, Philippa wrote underneath, 'Thank You, dear God. We have so many things to make days special.'

 God fills every day with good things.

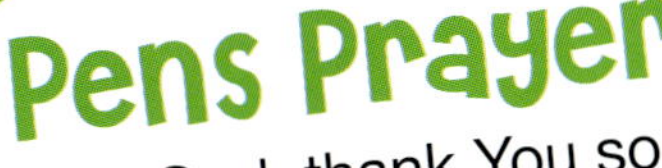

Pens Prayer

Lord God, thank You so much for the everyday things that make every day special. Amen.

Day 10

'… [Jesus] was met by ten men suffering from a dreaded skin disease.' (Luke 17 v 12)

Jesus was out walking. He was on His way to a big town called Jerusalem.

As He walked, He came to a village.

And that wasn't all.

In the distance were some men. Quite a lot of men. They were shuffling along slowly.

Jesus counted them.

'Ten,' He said to Himself. 'I wonder where they're off to all together.'

Jesus travelled a long way to teach as many people as He could about God.

Pens Prayer

Dear Lord Jesus, thank You so much that You once came to earth to live with us. You know just what it's like to be me. Amen.

'They stood at a distance and shouted, "Jesus! Master! Take pity on us!"' (Luke 17 v 12–13)

When the ten men spotted Jesus, they stopped.

'We'd better not come any closer,' one of them called.

Jesus stopped, too. He realised why they were keeping away from Him.

The men weren't well.

Not well at all.

They had a horrible skin disease and it was very easy to catch it. Every day they had to try to stay away from other people.

But today was different. Today was the day the ten men would meet Jesus.

They recognised Him straightaway.

'Dear Jesus!' they cried. 'Please help us! You can make us better.'

Jesus was very well known because of the wonderful things He said and did.

Pens Prayer

You've promised always to hear me when I call to You. Thank You, Jesus. Amen.

The Man Who Made Jesus Happy
Saying thank you matters

Day 12

'Jesus … said to them, "Go and let the priests examine you."' (Luke 17 v 14)

Jesus smiled at each of the ten men.

'They have such faith in God,' He thought to Himself. 'They know that I can make them better with His power.'

The ten men didn't move. They stood watching Jesus and waiting for something to happen.

Jesus didn't move either. He simply said, 'Go and look for a priest who serves God in the Temple. Ask him to have a good look at you. He'll be able to tell you if you're better or not.'

Jesus knew He had the power to make the sick men well.

Pens Prayer

Thank You, Jesus, for the amazing things You did that teach me to trust in God. Amen.

Day 13

'On the way they were made clean.'
(Luke 17 v 14)

The ten men glanced at each other. They didn't look any different. They didn't *feel* any different either. But they did as Jesus told them.

They went off to find a priest.

Jesus' eyes sparkled happily. He knew that something wonderful was about to happen.

And something wonderful did.

The very next time the men looked at each other, they could hardly believe their eyes.

'You're better!' cried one.

'So are you!' beamed another.

'We ALL are!' laughed a third.

Their skin was smooth again. The disease had gone.

'What a day!' they shouted joyfully. 'What a BRILLIANT day!'

God's power made the ten men better.

Pens Prayer

Dear Lord Jesus, whether I'm well or whether I'm ill, thank You that You never leave me. Amen.

The Man Who Made Jesus Happy
Saying thank you matters
Day 14
'When one of them saw that he was healed, he came back, praising God in a loud voice.'
(Luke 17 v 15)
The thankful man

The ten men were so excited, they hardly knew what to do with themselves. But they didn't all turn round and rush back to thank Jesus.

Only one of them did that.

'I must find Him!' he muttered to himself as he ran down the road.

At last the man spotted Him.

'Jesus!' he yelled. 'You did it, Jesus! You made us well. Look at me!'

Then he threw himself down onto the ground in front of Him.

'I don't know how to thank You,' the man murmured. 'You've changed my life for ever.'

Only one man realised how important it was to thank Jesus.

Pens Prayer

Amazing Jesus, God's Son, You love ME so much that You want to be part of my life. Thank You. Amen.

The Man Who Made Jesus Happy

Saying thank you matters

Day 15

'There were ten men who were healed; where are the other nine?' (Luke 17 v 17)

Jesus was pleased.

He was pleased to see the man looking so healthy.

He was pleased he'd come back to say thank you.

But when Jesus looked down the road, it was empty. The other nine men He'd made better were nowhere to be seen.

'Where are the rest of you?' Jesus asked the man who'd come to find Him. 'I healed ten of you today. Why haven't the other nine come to say thank you, too?'

Then He added kindly, 'My friend, because You trusted Me, You are well again. I'm glad you came back to see Me.'

Jesus deserves thanks every day because He helps us get close to our Father God.

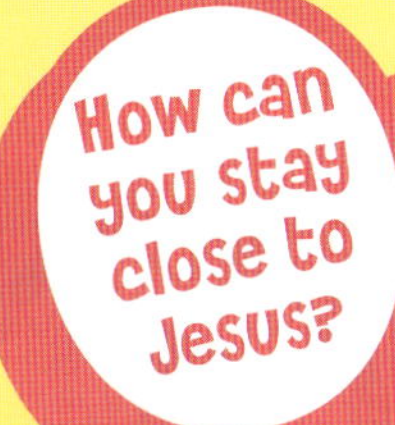

Pens Prayer

Loving Lord Jesus, I want to be full of thanks to You, today and every day. Amen.

GOD'S FAMILY

'Love one another warmly as Christian brothers and sisters, and be eager to show respect for one another.'
(Romans 12 v 10)

one big family

Squiggle and Splodge, the Scribble twins, did almost everything together.

They went for walks together; they ate their meals together.

They looked at books together; they played games together.

'If I didn't have Squiggle,' Splodge worried, 'I wouldn't know what to do.'

Charlotte smiled. 'Squiggle isn't your only family, Splodge,' she said. 'When we make friends with God, we become part of His family, as well.'

'Where does God's family live?' asked Splodge.

'All over the world,' Charlotte explained. 'God's family is HUGE. They all love God and God hopes that they will all love each other, too.'

God's friends all over the world are called 'the family of God'.

How many people are there in your own family? You can include grandparents, aunts, uncles and cousins.

Pens Prayer

Father God, You've invited me into Your family. Thank You that I am so special to You. Amen.

God's Family

'We always thank God for you all and always mention you in our prayers.' (1 Thessalonians 1 v 2)

Prayer for Philippa

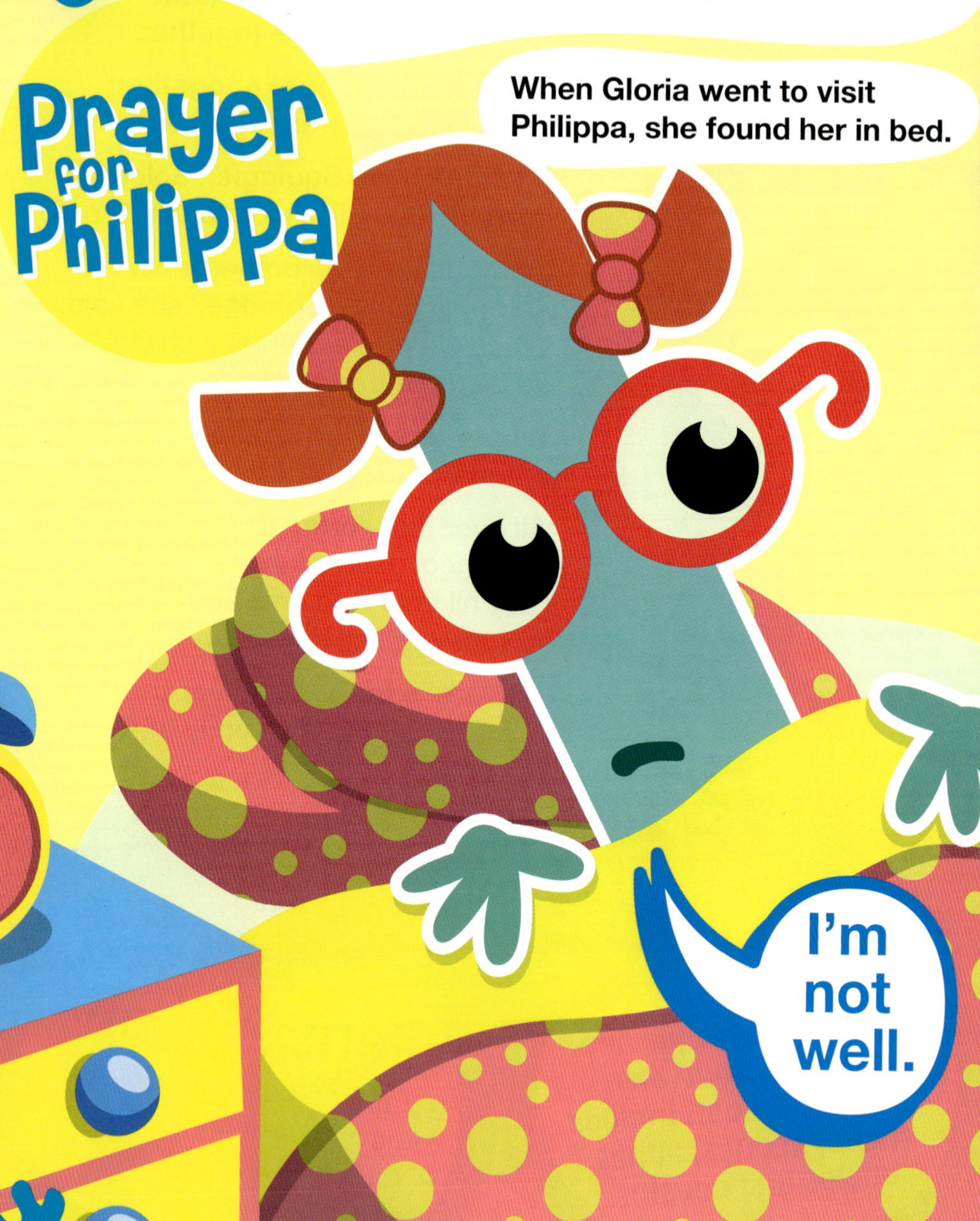

Gloria made sure that Philippa had a glass of water beside her bed for when she was thirsty, and some biscuits, too.

Then she said, 'I'm going to find Pens. We'll pray for you.'

Pens all thanked God for Philippa. She was such a good friend. Then they asked Him to help her feel better.

When Gloria visited the next day, Philippa smiled, 'Thank you so much, Gloria. It's helped me just knowing that you all care enough to pray for me.'

God's family can show their love by praying for one another.

Pens Prayer

Lord God, please help me remember to pray for those who might need Your extra special care. Amen.

'I praise the LORD, because he guides me ...'
(Psalm 16 v 7)

'What's that?'

Max bought a wooden bird table on a tall stand, with a little roof over the top.

'Perfect,' he smiled, putting it on his lawn.

Sharpy wasn't so sure.

'What's that?' he wondered, just a tiny bit scared. 'It's very tall and thin, and has a VERY odd-shaped head.'

He crouched down and, 'Grrr!' he growled.

'Don't worry, Sharpy,' Max laughed. 'It's just a bird table. Come on. I'll show you it's quite safe.'

God hopes His family will help each other if they're worried about anything.

Pens Prayer

Loving Lord, when I need help, I want to be ready to ask for it. When someone else needs help, I want to be ready to give it. Amen.

39

God's Family

'You are the people of God; he loved you and chose you for his own.' (Colossians 3 v 12)

Marco's helper

'Yes, please,' answered Marco. 'But I'm not sure what to wash it with.'

'We can use my special sponge,' said Denzil.

'And the tyres need more air,' Marco went on, 'but my pump's broken.'

'You can borrow mine,' replied Denzil.

'The pedals are squeaking, too,' added Marco, 'and I haven't got any oil.'

'I have,' smiled Denzil.

Soon Marco's bike was looking like new.

'Thank you so much, Denzil,' beamed Marco. 'I don't know what I'd have done without you.'

 Being part of God's family means caring and sharing.

Pens Prayer

Dear God, thank You for the love You show to Your family. Please help me to love them, too. Amen.

God's Family

'No more shouting or insults, no more hateful feelings of any sort.' (Ephesians 4 v 31)

The colour quarrel

'My bedroom needs painting,' Charlotte said to Gloria one day. 'Will you help me choose the colour, please?'

Gloria suggested pink then purple; blue then yellow; orange then green. But Charlotte wasn't sure any of those colours would look right.

'If you don't like my ideas,' snapped Gloria, 'then why did you ask me to help you?'

'It's your fault,' grumbled Charlotte. 'You're saying the wrong things.'

'No, I'm not!' shouted Gloria. '*You're* just being silly!'

'Why are you quarrelling?' Philippa asked. 'Whatever's wrong, I'm sure you can sort it out without speaking unkindly to each other.'

God doesn't like quarrels. He wants His family to live together happily.

Pens Prayer

Father God, I'm sorry for times when I speak crossly. I want to try to speak kindly always. Amen.

Day 21
God's Family
'Teach and instruct each other with all wisdom.'
(Colossians 3 v 16)
What is God's love like?
44

Splodge was wondering.

'What's God's love like?' she asked Squiggle.

'Let's ask,' Squiggle answered.

Philippa said, 'It's like a cool drink of water when you're thirsty.'

Max said, 'It's like tasty food when you're hungry.'

Charlotte said, 'It's like the best song you've ever heard.'

Denzil said, 'It's like laughter you can't help joining in with.'

Gloria said, 'It's like a snugly blanket when it's cold.'

Marco said, 'It's like the biggest hug when you're feeling sad.'

'Thank you all!' cried Splodge. 'Now we know exactly what God's love is like. It's like EVERYTHING THAT MAKES YOU FEEL BETTER.'

 God's family can help each other get to know Him.

Who can you ask if you have any questions about God?

Pens Prayer

Thank You, dear Lord, that through other people in Your family I can learn more about You. Amen.

Day 22 God's Family

'Lord, if my brother keeps on sinning against me, how many times do I have to forgive him?' (Matthew 18 v 21)

max's new skate-board

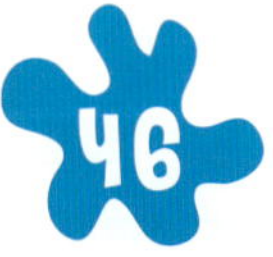

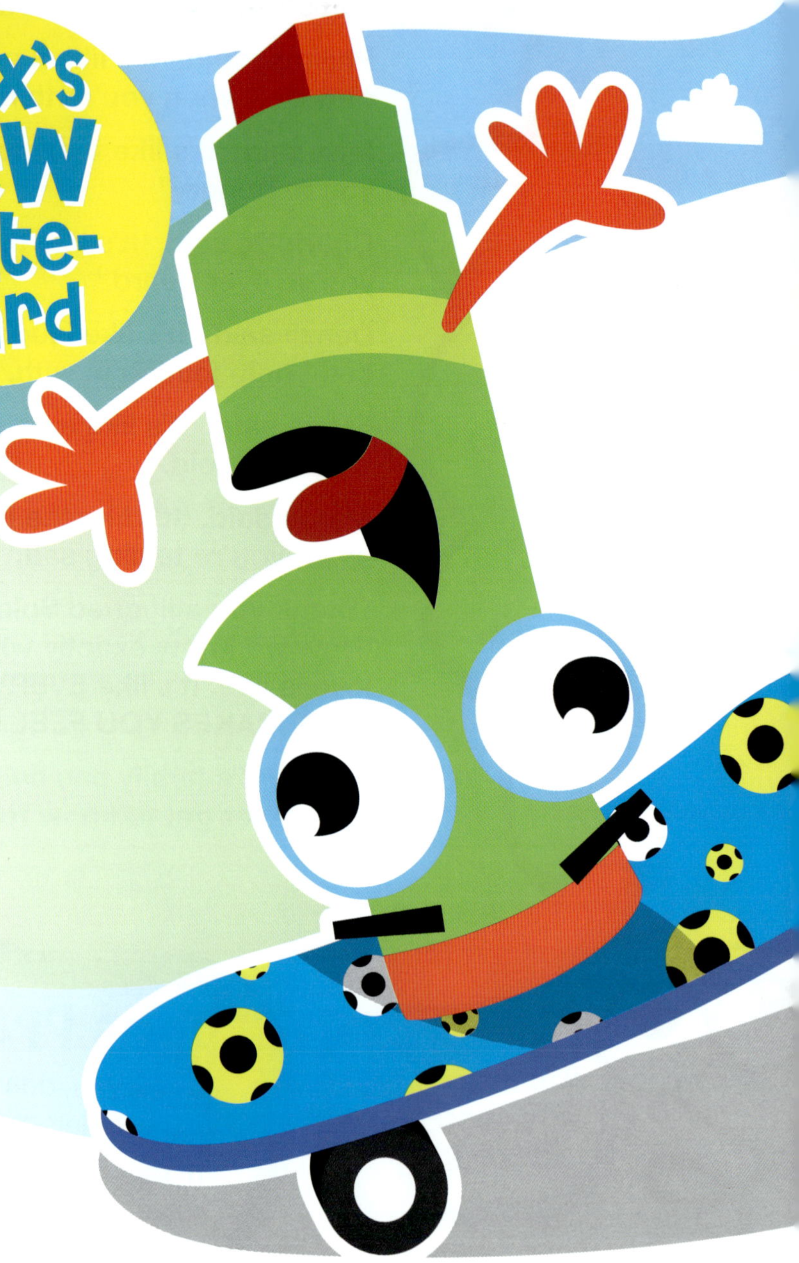

Max had a brand-new skateboard.

'May I have a go, please?' asked Marco.

'Of course,' said Max. 'But go slowly. I'd hate it to get broken.'

Marco zoomed along.

'Slow down,' called Max.

'I *am* going slowly,' Marco called back.

'Not so fast!' shouted Max.

'I'm *not* going fast!' Marco shouted back.

Then it happened. He crashed, and the skateboard broke.

'Now look what you've done!' yelled Max.

'I'll get you another one,' mumbled Marco. 'I'm really sorry.'

'You're *always* sorry,' Max muttered, 'but I forgive you. I just wish you'd listened to me in the first place.'

 God keeps forgiving His family when they do bad things. His family need to keep forgiving each other, too.

Sometimes forgiving someone can seem hard. Who can you ask to help you?

Pens Prayer

Heavenly Father, when someone upsets me and makes me sad, please help me to be ready to forgive them. Amen.

'So we are to use our different gifts in accordance with the grace that God has given us.' (Romans 12 v 6)

Denzil had been to see a puppet show.

'That was brilliant!' he said excitedly. 'I'm going to make some puppets of my own.'

Denzil thought finger puppets would be the easiest to make. He found some cloth and some wool, but wasn't at all sure what to do with them.

'I'll ask Gloria to help,' he decided. 'She knows all about making things.'

Gloria showed Denzil how to cut the puppet shapes out and sew them together. Sewing was what Gloria was best at.

'You're so clever, Gloria,' beamed Denzil. 'Thank you for showing me what to do.'

 God hopes His family will share the things they are good at with each other.

What sort of things do you make at your school or preschool?

Pens Prayer

Thank You for the gifts You've given me, Lord God. I always want to be ready to share them. Amen.

God's Family

'Go, then, to all peoples everywhere and make them my disciples …' (Matthew 28 v 19)

Talking about God

I don't know. Without our Pens friends, we might not know how much He loves us.

'Exactly,' Squiggle went on. 'That's why all of us who know God need to try and talk about Him with others who don't.'

'That'll make God happy, won't it?' said Splodge thoughtfully. 'He wants everyone everywhere to know He loves them.'

God wants His friends to tell others about Him so that people everywhere can be part of His family.

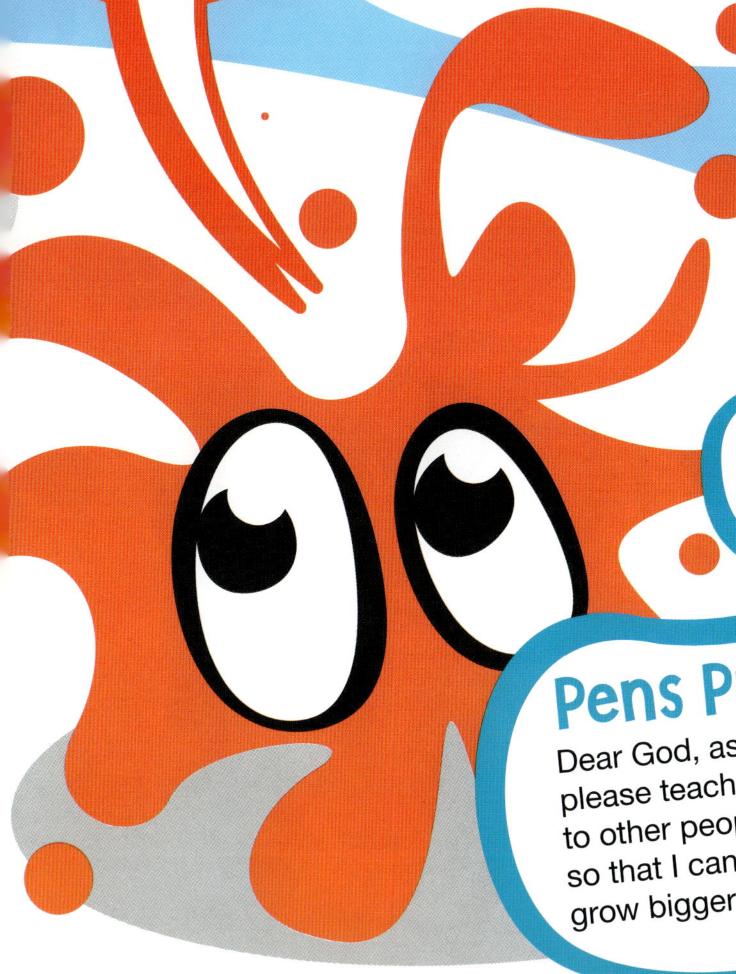

Who talks to you about God?

Pens Prayer

Dear God, as I grow bigger, please teach me how to talk to other people about You so that I can help Your family grow bigger, too. Amen.

'Praise the LORD, all living creatures!' (Psalm 150 v 6)

Charlotte had just learnt a new song of praise to God. She was singing it in her garden.

'May I join in?' Denzil asked.

'Of course,' Charlotte replied.

They hadn't been singing for long when Max, Marco, Philippa and Gloria arrived.

'We heard your song,' Philippa said. 'Please may we sing it with you?'

Pens opened their mouths and out came Charlotte's beautiful new song of praise to God.

'I'm sure God liked this song when I was singing it by myself,' Charlotte smiled. 'But I expect He loves it even more now we're all praising Him together!'

 God loves to hear His family praising Him.

Pens Prayer

Father, I praise You that I can be a special part of Your family for ever. Amen.

'… the younger son sold his part of the property and left home with the money.' (Luke 15 v 13)

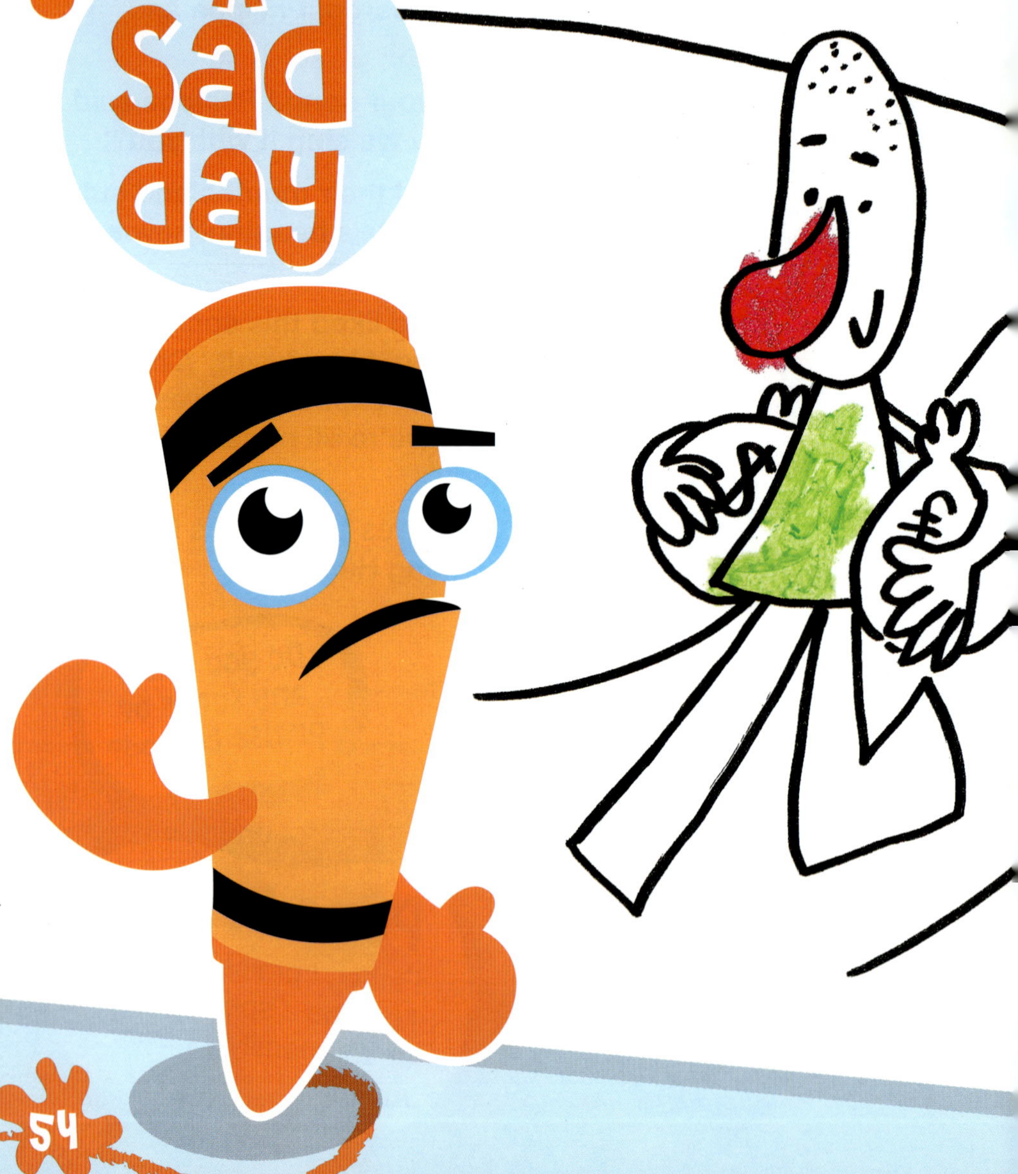

Jesus was teaching people how much God loves them and wants them to be part of His family.

He told a story about a man and his two sons.

The younger son was very selfish. He said to his father unkindly, 'One day, everything you own and all your money will belong to my brother and to me. I don't want to live with you any more. I want my share now.'

The father decided to give him what he asked for. Then, feeling very sad because he loved his son so much, he watched him leave the family home.

Just like the selfish son's father, God is sad when we choose to live our lives without Him.

Pens Prayer

Father God, I'm sorry if there are times when I do selfish things that make You sad. Amen.

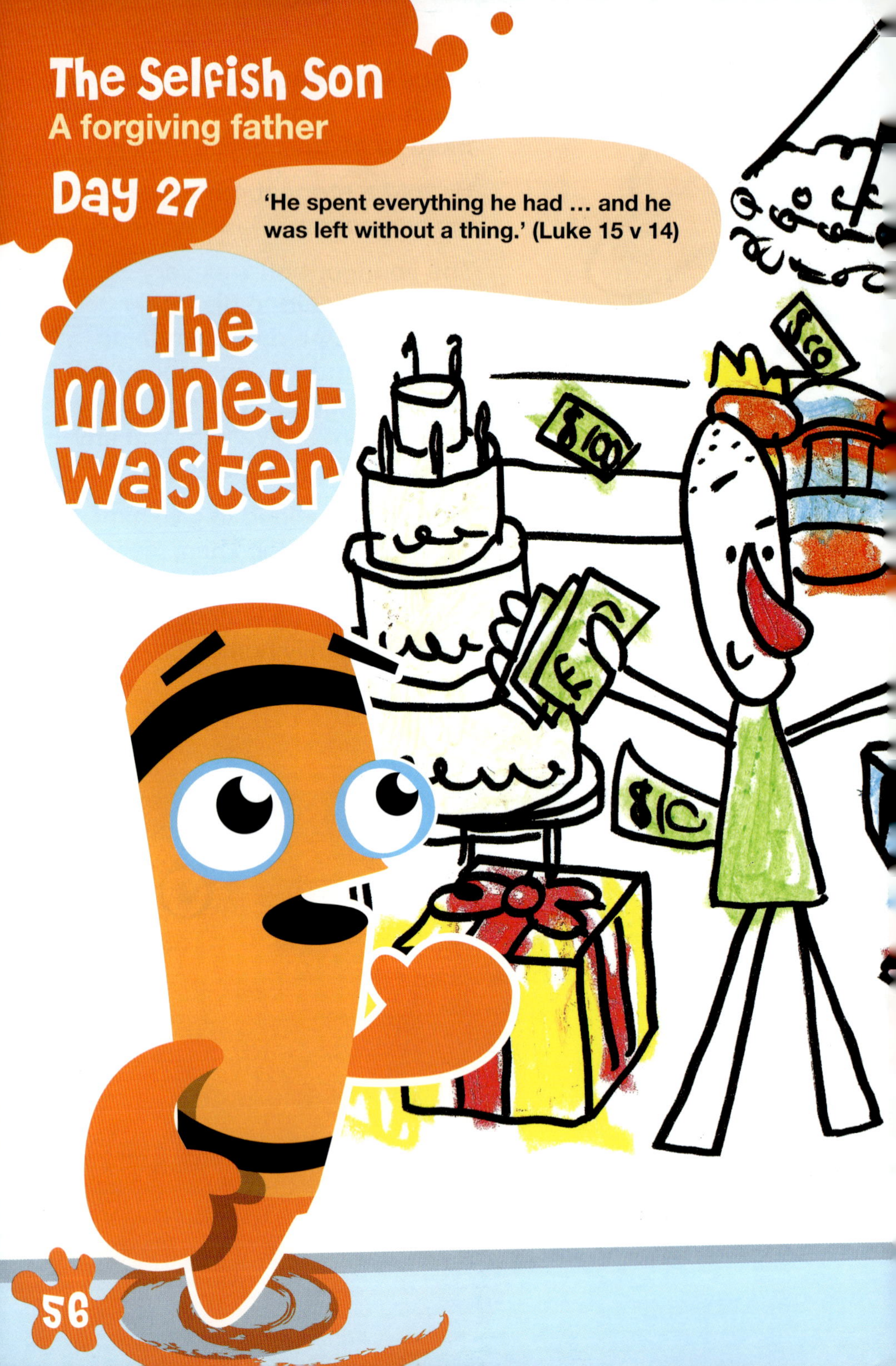
The Selfish Son
A forgiving father
Day 27
'He spent everything he had … and he was left without a thing.' (Luke 15 v 14)
The money-waster
56

The selfish son was very excited to have lots of money.

'Now I can do exactly as I like,' he said to himself. 'I can spend my money where I want, whenever I want.'

He set off, and travelled a long way from his family home.

But, instead of using his money carefully, he wasted it. He bought things he didn't need and things that were bad for him.

One day, the selfish son had nothing left.

'What am I going to do now?' he wondered miserably. 'I'll have to find a job to earn some more money.'

The selfish son behaved badly and ended up with nothing.

Pens Prayer

Dear Lord, please hold my hand every day and help me to live the way You want me to. Amen.

Day 28

'I will get up and go to my father …' (Luke 15 v 18)

An idea

The selfish son went to work on a farm. It was his job to look after the pigs.

But no one gave him any food. Some days he was so hungry that he felt like gobbling up what the pigs were eating.

'I've never felt so miserable in all my life,' he groaned. 'The people who work for my father have plenty of food and I'm sitting here starving!'

That's when he made up his mind.

'I'll go home,' he decided. 'I'll tell my father I'm sorry for being so stupid. Perhaps he'll let me work for him.'

The selfish son realised that leaving his family was a big mistake.

Pens Prayer

Loving Father, thank You that when I'm sorry for the wrong things I do\ You always forgive me. Amen.

The Selfish Son
A forgiving father
Day 29
'… [his father] ran, threw his arms round his son, and kissed him.' (Luke 15 v 20)
Home
60

The selfish son had to walk a long way to get home.

'Who's that?' he wondered when he was still quite far away.

A man was running towards him.

'It can't be …' the son murmured. 'It is! MY FATHER!'

'MY SON!' his father cried, giving him a HUGE hug. 'I've been looking out for you every day!'

'I'm so sorry,' sobbed his son. 'I've been stupid and selfish. I'm too bad to be called your son any more.'

'Of course you're my son!' laughed his father. 'I love you and I've missed you so much. Welcome home.'

 The selfish son had made his father very sad, but his father never stopped loving him.

Pens Prayer

Lord God, Your love for me is always patient and kind. I praise You! Amen.

The Selfish Son
A forgiving father

Day 30

'… your brother … was lost, but now he has been found.' (Luke 15 v 32)

A loving father

62

At home, the father fetched smart clothes and shoes for his son. Then he arranged a 'Welcome Home' party.

When the son's older brother came back from work, he asked, 'What's the party for?'

A servant told him, and the brother was angry.

'Father!' he shouted. 'My selfish brother went off and was stupid. Why are you being kind to him?'

'Listen,' smiled his father. 'You live with me and everything that's mine belongs to you. But your brother went away. I didn't know where he was. Now he's safely home! We *had* to have a party!'

Like a father welcoming a lost child, God jumps for joy whenever someone new joins God's family!

Pens Prayer

Heavenly Father, what You want most of all is for EVERYONE to be part of Your family. Thank You for Your amazing love. Amen.

Pens titles

More *Pens* for you to enjoy

- ★ Friends
- ★ Father God
- ★ Following Jesus
- ★ Really Special
- ★ Trusting God
- ★ Helping and Serving
- ★ Big and Small
- ★ God's Book
- ★ God's Love
- ★ God Cares
- ★ God's Heroes
- ★ Thank You God

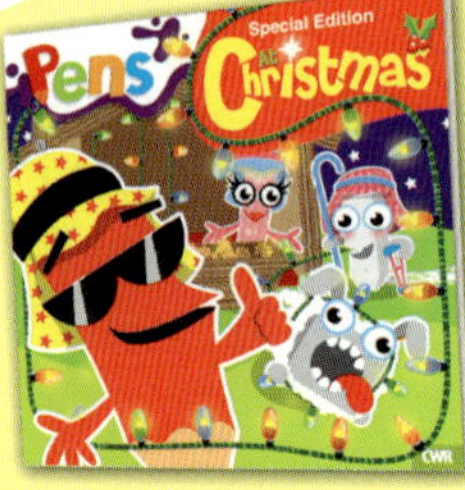

Pens Special!
Christmas

The *Pens* characters tell the Christmas story to make Jesus' birth real and memorable for young children, also with five days of Bible-reading notes.

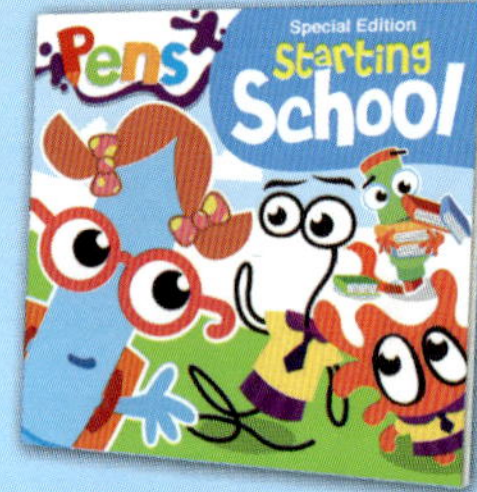

Pens Special!
Starting School

Help children start school confidently, knowing that God goes there with them. A short story followed by five days of Bible notes.

For current prices visit
www.cwr.org.uk/store

Available online, or from your local Christian bookshop.

**Coming January 2012:
Pens Special! Easter**

OTHER CWR DAILY BIBLE-READING NOTES
Every Day with Jesus for adults
Inspiring Women Every Day for women
Lucas on Life Every Day for adults
Cover to Cover Every Day for adults
Mettle for 14- to 18-year-olds
YP's for 11- to 15-year-olds
Topz for 7- to 11-year-olds

Ideal for children aged 3 to 6

Come on in and meet your Pen friends! Together we'll find out about the good things God give us each day, and about helping others to join His family.

Join us as we draw you closer to God every day through our stories Bible readings and prayers.

www.cwr.org.uk

ISBN 978-1-85345-633-6

9 781853 456336

Tel: 01252 784700   Email: mail@cwr.org.uk

CWR
Applying God's Word
to everyday life and relationships

CLC
ME 3·99p

Pens
Thank YOU God
Daily devotions for young children
CWR

Introducing
Pens

Gloria Glitter-pen
She's fabulously fashionable and adores hats. A bit of a fusspot maybe, but still there for a friend in need.

Charlotte Chalk
Cheerful and chirpy, she loves to sing! She's always happy to join in the fun whatever the day brings.

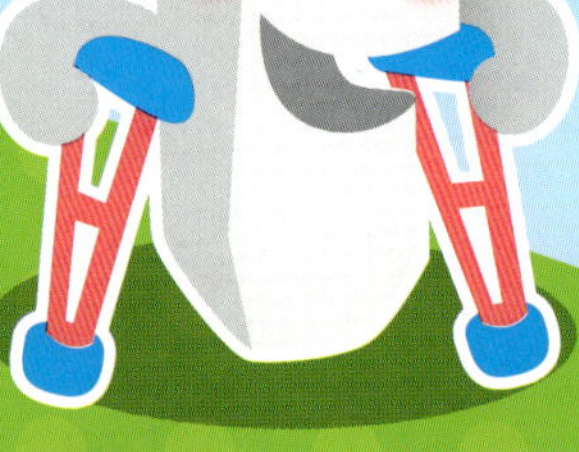

Denzil the Pencil
He's definitely the King of Cool, although perhaps not always as confident as he likes to make out.

Sharpy
He's lively, he's loveable, he knows how to get himself in a mess – and he's Pens' very best friend.